THE NATIONAL POETRY SERIES

The National Poetry Series was established in 1978 to ensure the publication of five poetry books annually through participating publishers. Publication is funded by the late James Michener, the Copernicus Society of America, Edward J. Piszek, the Lannan Foundation, and the Tiny Tiger Foundation.

2001 COMPETITION WINNERS

Betsy Brown of Minneapolis, Minnesota, *Year of Morphines*
Selected by George Garrett, to be published by
Louisiana State University Press

David Groff of New York, New York, *Theory of Devolution*
Selected by Mark Doty, to be published by University of Illinois Press

Terrance Hayes of Pittsburgh, Pennsylvania, *Hip Logic*
Selected by Cornelius Eady, to be published by Viking Penguin

Elizabeth Robinson of Berkeley, California, *The Tunnel*
Selected by Fanny Howe, to be published by Sun & Moon Press

Ruth Schwartz of Oakland, California, *Edgewater*
Selected by Jane Hirshfield, to be published by HarperCollins

YEAR OF MORPHINES

p o e m s

Betsy Brown

Louisiana State University Press

Baton Rouge

First printing

11 10 09 08 07 06 05 04 03 02

5   4   3   2   1

Designer: Amanda McDonald Scallan
Typeface: Sabon
Printer and binder: Thomson-Shore, Inc.

Library of Congress Cataloging-in-Publication Data

Brown, Betsy.
    Year of morphines : poems / Betsy Brown.
        p. cm.
    ISBN 0-8071-2782-5 (cloth : alk. paper) — ISBN 0-8071-2783-3)pbk. : alk. paper)
    I. Title.

    PS3602.R67 Y43 2002
    811'.6—dc21
                                                    2001050352

The author gratefully acknowledges the editors of the following publications, in which some of the poems
herein first appeared, sometimes in slightly different form: *American Poetry Review:* "Dignity in the
Home," "It Never Comes Out of Nowhere," "Necedah, Wisconsin—12/24/96," "Rage"; *Black Warrior Re-
view:* "Formica Road"; *Cimarron Review:* "Landlords, We Don't Just Disappear into Those Homes"; *Col-
lege English:* "Endo," "It Might Be Deep Blue," "The Mirror to Deal With," "Other Math," "Rivera Live
at Cyrano's," "Ruthless Use of Men as Dictionaries"; *Denver Quarterly:* "Music," "Wisconsin"; *River-
wind:* "Mary Magdalene Talks to Jesus on Holy Thursday," "In Memoriam," "Summer"; *Seneca Review:*
"No Deliberate Tributary"; *Sonora Review:* "This Pulls on Choice."

For Maggy Brown

1965–1998

. . . that flat, sandpapered look the sky gets
Out in the middle west toward the end of summer,
The look of wanting to back out before the argument
Has been resolved, and at the same time to save appearances
So that tomorrow will be pure.
　　　—John Ashbery

Contents

I

Wisconsin

The world pulls back off from you like a camera moving
out into the universe aimed at you, you're still
in the phone booth while it ascends, you're calling
the ringing, you saw his brother behind him
the chair crash into his head
you think you saw this, he was crying, his brother
other times but not this way
from back, the phone
still rings now and the camera is recording
you, panning back, the cinematographer hoped
the moment was instant, caught him after
the floor was in pieces, someone
has gone insane, he never speaks,
the record of it quickly violently embarrassing like
a dream you had while you sweat holes through July
that caught you, you wanted one thing completely
briefly, beyond you, the weight of 11 o'clock
11 rings, they tore down the lake with condos,
no one was watching the boys left
the 13-year-old girl passed out in the snow
her cinematographer was Chance—she nailed it
and the air grows cold in the same circle you forget
surrounding the phone booth pulling away always,
the highway in the blizzard littered with jackknifed
semis like horses, they didn't find
out about you, you believe this somewhere
you try through the ringing to stop, through winter
to be the kind of person who'd fall in love.
He is gentle drinking tequila, was he?, and
the night is a lesbian, drunk
hanging all over a man, calling him Baby . . .
night waiting for something that calls upon violence—
your unflagging unpinning of all intercourse human—
night a goddess flashed through this belief:
It is actually other than this.

The cinematographer of another order, leaves begin to cover
the booth—Take this. Light a candle.
It is more evening than this somewhere else.
Your ancient landscape and a woman weeps
before Mary in the church in a circle forever
because it never, once, got okay. Get
your slews ready to go. It comes
in an instant and it's all different now, you
will go gladly to Nebraska and never say
Where have I just been? The house simply
disappeared and the children went another place
to grow a tenderness they never told the story of,
recorded outside themselves by a tone
they never learned the language of, the tone
in a lake black in autumn, the drowned boy kissing
the dock in his life jacket and the ones who screamed Fuck
too late. It moves away.
The faith is out there somewhere,
the cold training slaps you up and you're
just like you thought you were.
The awful science in how purely the sun sets,
the sun comes up all over your head out of nowhere—this—
this would be good lighting for a shot
wouldn't it? Take me now?
It's so far away the earth is beautiful swirly
unkempt and childlike without system
but filmed and they do know—
they know all about it.

Formica Road

I take Route 21
to Oshkosh all year through
quilt terrain, horse-
drawn Amish buggies

parked in the driveway
of the shop closed
on Sundays near
the spent stone farmhouse,

the girl who sold me
hickory nuts with her
St. Bernard, through
heaping winters, led

only by my love
for the moon. When
you died they put us
on a detour. Well.

When you were sick I tried
stitching you one square—
Tumbling Blocks in
velvet from sliced-up dresses

on sale, by hand each
dark diamond starred
clean, scar-sterile
gauze filled pocket—

I didn't finish. Detour
ran through good sod
land, prime source
of baler twine. I watched

a girl waiting to cross
21, huge aluminum
mailbox and her hip
out, her elbow cocked;

she thought the boy, *the*
boy, might pass in his
Trans Am. Wave, girl.
All these passages back:

Tomah, Coloma, Wautoma,
the driveway I tried to reach
my star of wonder and got
a swaddling babe, gurneys,

IV lines, tiles and
skin, the smell of hot
Styrofoam at seven, eight
separate lines, Sweetie,

feeding your heart directly.
Nobody sings much now
when I cross Formica Road.
Could we have sewn in my own

heart? It might seem like
the middle of nowhere out here
but this way is a shortcut,
the truncated gravel just scars.

Rage

In 1764, a herding dog lunged out
of her fields to ravage the French village
of Thiers, attacking 20 people

and infecting them fiercely with
pre-Pasteurian rabies, called *rage*
by the French. You traveled to Paris

to study the original printings
of these stories: the victims doomed,
the pages onionskin parchment

too frail to copy, sometimes too precious
to open, the bitten first numbed
with knowing what's coming, then,

as they say, enraged, terrified of water,
convulsant, apologetic about how much
they wanted to bite their Parisian

doctor, who bled them and burned
the fanged gouges with steel and mercury.
In the Fifth Arrondissement, your

fine tall library, your walk daily through
Luxembourg gardens and all the slim
streets past high black iron gates,

shuttered windowpanes; they put
the victims in a huge vacant hospice
and separated those who became

hydrophobic: *Eh Monsieur, I see clearly
that I am lost, they place me in this
unfortunate room, from which no one returns.*

In 18th century France, *rage* patients
sought miracle cures at the shrine
of St.-Hubert, the priests worked

to keep that pilgrimage active,
and all the scholars fought about
the passions and the morals of the dead.

I'm sorry I had to take you home
from Paris. It was snowing and you
were crying. All the mad strangled

rabid patients carried us, remember,
back to Baltimore; you wanted
to save them, we brought our offerings

to radiologists, we applied to oncologists—
we were all ghosts and stories
about walks to the health-food store

and the ways people so deeply numbed
find to talk about a future. In Thiers,
the 12-year-old boy just simply

could not drink the water. He shattered
the cup and convulsed so violently
they tied him to the bed. Tonight

in a tiny lamplit apartment in Paris,
a reader sits riveted by the newspaper—
all these stories ending with life.

Famous Tiaras

Bright plastic beads, hearts, stars, sparks,
baubles, dripping down threads blazed to the waist,

snug around an ankle in Vegas, in D.C.,
on doorknobs in Baltimore with cowbells loud clunky for

each visitor, children's charms easily restrung,
flares of pearls, kitschy pop song of gems,

amulets too light for luck. I look here a lot.
Lake Superior prime glowing agate forest,

all the junk-shop rhinestone buttons in Hampden,
your charm bracelet, mine, scorched mushroom pendant,

the class picture, a boy's St. Christopher medal,
a FedEx'd crystal or from my raincoat pocket

the last little disk of jewelry you wore. Let's
throw it off the dock like mist and kindling.

Year of Morphines

Baltimore black winter rain,
the doorbell buzzed, we stayed
on your friends' foldout couch

during your treatments, drawn back
to this city of doctors, messy brain scans,
slick cobblestoned lanes thick

with Christmas, pulled into cold drizzle
like all the last vigils we knew
but now for us, the sleet, the complicated locks,

people dropped off papers, they brought
chick peas. This 19th-century parlor
on Bolton Hill gone bad, I kept

your drugs hidden. The shutters above
our bed rose two stories, your two a.m.
dose sometimes flew, we were barefoot

with grapefruit when the head of your
department stopped with your mail, I knew
I had the stillborn face of family—

numb daze and sorry sleep. The summer
before, in Duluth, a girl drank pure morphine
at a bonfire. She died the strangled

creep of dreams a 14-year-
old sees slower and dozy, no last
phone call to say Should I go

to the emergency? I listened our year
of morphines. I would hear you today
if you rustled those waters slyly

where you snuggle now. I learned
once it takes 20 minutes
for downers to work, 20 weeks

for traumatic shock. In Baltimore the rain
slides in through cracks like ice to stifle
final dreamy mornings, cold alarm.

Endo

It doesn't really matter the exact speed
at the time of impact; the motorcycle won't
flip forward from the front wheel
if it's not moving at a certain fast-
enough rate. What's
crucial, then, is that it flip front wheel
over back back over front
a couple of times to qualify
as an endo. And
it doesn't matter really what the rider does—
the endo has to do with the motion in the air
of the bike
through the air frontward
along the same path the bike was aimed at
forward originally before
impact, the straight line for travel
maintained through probably
the first revolution, endwise,
of the machine so that it might
appear that it might—
from midair appear—
continue by its machination alone
down the highway
of its own will, wherever it would—
sustaining the hundred miles an hour
it flips at, the midair moment
the will is created like someone's head
smashing on your head
at a hundred miles an hour only
in that moment
what it lands on, end
over end over
the rider or on,
the rider who must become
air, who must become more
than the road we take, must become

faster and farther than the bike,
who must move more, become now
more than where we work who we fuck
how we get there forever
world without world
through air end over
and ever.

Necedah, Wisconsin—12/24/96

21 degrees below zero the air is at attention creaking
in the blank lot of a Mobil station in central Wisconsin.

The stars crash and clatter through the richness of black sky like this
and then the huge moon orange like the dance I'll dance again

like all the dancers I envision having better gowns
better lighting lighter drinks. These woods are for Valium.

It doesn't much do to chew on this sting. A lone driver there,
headlights oncoming now as more and wiser souls head

to all our heartland bars; the smoky beerstung mouth of what
a home it gets made into, wake me from this floor leave me

alongside this pool table. I remember something.
I guess I should be lookin for Jesus.

It might be simply freezing, but I sure wish you never left.
I hang my scarf from the stop sign to whip you hello.

Greeting the Visitors

I looked for foxes my whole life. As a child
we lived across from a meadow where I heard

they ran. I never saw one but pictured the flash
of red on snow, the smart tilt of ears; ah, how

a child wants to see a fox. In Baltimore, you take
what you can get. You can walk here for days in rain.

I think I hear the phone ring. I think it's time,
it might be now that the glimpse gets through. Do you

recognize me from anything? I'm not hiding behind
this apron, but no one will look at my face. The mother

fox is a fool; she hides her kits. Look—a stringy vixen
with a dead rat in her mouth, crossing the street in Baltimore.

No one needs me right now, I guess. Good-bye.
I'll just be in the corner slitting my wrists.

Midwest Boys

In Oshkosh, Wisconsin,
we kept it in mind
I-41 went clear down

to Florida. These scoop-necked
midsized midwestern
towns, set up separate originally

on waterways for trading—
first furs, then lumber,
the workers drinkers

voiceless then fierce
for the hell of it, tense
machinery, construction.

As a teenager you noted
mainly the routes out.
Spring, the dead mud,

the bad paint job, drifting jarred
eaves troughs, sullen pickup
sunk to its axles on the lawn.

A boy's mind turns to the road.
Tract houses, one, one,
all along the frontage road

with tequila and Old Style, pot,
cheap speed; if you're
a girl you try to remember:

They shoved candlesticks
up Linda. They drew on her
with her Bonne Bell.

If you pass out
they'll strip you,
you won't know

and if you're lucky only
photograph you. These pictures
show up on bulletin boards.

In Eau Claire, 1992, teenage
boys dropped rocks from
an overpass over I-94,

aiming for windshields.
Martin Blommer in his
Winnebago, hit by a 32-

pound rock; his wife alongside
didn't hear it, the crash,
the RV veered in a second

into the median, staggering
to stop, and he, in silence,
transfixed instantly, forever.

32 pounds. These are
my highways. I remember.
Long-play radio stations,

driving in moonlight
past hours of white
white mute fields.

I never wanted
to go back to Florida.
As a girl I didn't

have much to compare—
dime bags, shot glasses, lives
that trudged with losses

and butane. I can't forgive them.
Where could one drunk girl
find an ocean?

In the first forced blink of spring
I hate you.
I remember your names.

My curse on you is this:
May you have daughters
and may you love them.

Minneapolis in January

They set up the steel frames
and girders for the apartment building
at the north end of Lake Calhoun,

crept in and hung on like a blizzard,
slow to begin but then one day we started
to really like the cranes. Two towers

hoisting steel over these inner-city
lakes like cranky pterodactyls.
Seven below for your daily walk,

and me alongside. I told you: You have to
know the lake paths, they're tricky;
it seems foolproof, but no—the lure

of warmer neighborhoods, some side road
beyond the grid and all the hidden
strange lakes; you can end up anywhere.

Our brother spotted the cranes on his visit—
You could see them from everywhere:
15 stories high, half a block long;

I saw that complex go up,
fill out, get glass and lights
and walls. The people moved in

at Thanksgiving: model showrooms
with chairs and a torchère posed.
Then real people, giant red wreaths,

couches, glass statues, bikes
on the balconies and potted plants soaking
all that frozen light. They live there now.

The cranes are gone. I think about them.
I think sometimes that would be a cool job:
not to drive the cranes, but the job

to determine the scope of these projects.
What if they'd failed somehow
to finish those homes? It's perfect—

the kind of work where you know for sure
if you're doing it wrong. I'm sorry
about everything, you know. In winter

now, I carry a map. When I walk it's quiet
and I watch for the path we should have found—
the way home I owe you and don't know.

II

Easter

1

Two girls bareback
on a small bay horse,
quick head, long mane,
August Wisconsin sun
draped like a wool shawl
on halter tops, strong thighs,
easy reins. Blackbird calls

strict across cornfields,
blacktop sticks; Buck takes
the shoulder. Just over
the Soo Line tracks
a hickory grove narrows
to divide the fields.
The girls cross the road

casual down the edgeline
to the rise on the west side;
a sandpit drops sharp
to a pond deep below.
They never knew it was there.
12 and 14, the sisters split a joint
among the trees, a hawk

rides the thermals in silence.
They watch this prairie.
They have been told.
They don't yet know what grief is.
The wind rustling across the corn
is familiar, and the bay sweats
fine dirt a curved line

down their legs, he twitches
flies away. They know
how he'll move before he does.
The girls are linked like
strolling. Canvas shoes,
interchangeable hands.
Are you ready to recognize

this has become a lifetime?
There is nothing in this hearing
that makes sense but loss—
and they will lose.
The hawk has spied something
and she will dive.
The girls turn back to the day.

They will find rusty gates to close,
quarrels to lose, the sad escapes
of children at a dead run over dust.
This field is the beginning
of their native land.
This place of ghosts
where they hear someone weeping.

2
Because my mother and my sister died
both on Easter, 16 years apart,

I still look to see who rose those days
when the predawn blackness finally brought light

to their same sorry morphine crawl,
the glow that drew them then, Jesus Christ,

into peace, the same lost breast the slow
chemo-scarred veins and silence facing

refused final conversations. My mother Mary
Kay, 43, my sister Maggy, 32.

What stone rolled back on our Easters?
Who strolled the roads greeting old friends

and forced through some promise, now,
that will be kept, for Mary Kay, and Maggy?

3
Driving straight into the storm
with the sun setting behind me

the orange dank light backwashes
you my sunshine my man,

hey Judas check and see
if I have a halo. You're staring at

these trees, the pulpy remnants
of logs and height. Never

thought you'd have to deal
with me again. See

there are ways to stay
in motion: flight boards, crystals,

the bunny trail, chick peas,
don't give me that look,

antioxidants, aromatherapy,
Ophelia's flowers, the sporadic

love of a cheating man. Whom
did I ever kiss good-bye?

For you the storm stays off
dark ahead, formal. I

drive this road like the tide.
You don't know how much.

Well there are things to be done.
I am 36 fucking years old and all

this time I've been waiting for you?
Where did all the riverbanks go?

What is happening to this rain?
Okay this very second I'm running,

I'll reach the top here and dance
twirling naked on top of Knapp Hill

for you. I lost my Levi's
somewhere outside of Menomonie,

I spin over this Potter's Field—
above this green sleep I see clear

to that place I was born, east,
and back over the Mississippi to the west

where, dear god, I'm not yet dying.
It's so green, so globed and beautiful—

you are coming to me;
I have kept myself for you.

I've scattered shirts and body parts
across these rolling lazy hills,

the ashes of my family, my girls—
was it, really, for you

the lolling round tempo of grief?
Will they hang me in effigy too,

twisting creaking in the wind above
these famous trees on Knapp Hill?

How many pieces am I paying?
I would leap over the last flames of you

for luck, for life. I'm waiting
you bastard; I swore. I swore it.

4
It's the back of your neck
that warns you, the chill
stop at the base of your skull

that feels the shock of it, the drop
you're not going to make it;
this is the drape coming down,

the dense velvet pooled, I'm sorry,
in this ash, manic
plunge and you're simply afraid

that it might end. Did you
forget what spring
feels like? The trees are flush

for you, a central nervous
system of sprinkling
and ransoms. I don't have

any more room for flowers.
I can't be awake.
Take the bracelets and veils.

Give them to my secret
replacement, and watch.
I don't have any part of this.

5
It would be simpler to think
of martyrs and heroes if I

were better at math. The spring
purge, the rebirth, some Adonis

deserting that winter death
of Persephone; oh sorry, the charmed

life, the saving, shelving the sly
humblings of age. Three of us

are left. We take the shuttle,
my two sisters and I, to Newgrange

in Brú na Bóinne north of Dublin
to the passage tomb built 5,000

years ago by Neolithic farmers
to bury three New Stone Age neighbors

with a roof box at the entryway
that illuminates the tomb every year

at winter solstice. We crouch through
the gray passage to the cruciform

tomb, the tour guide turns out
the lights to simulate the day

the light begins to return
to these farm lands, that the new

possibility of a next chapter
starts, and the pinpoint of light

reaches our tourist eyes and rises,
flows, floods the cavern with its

three inlets for whomever it was
they lost back then, prehistory,

we're thinking of caving,
we're reading the graffiti

carved in the 18th century—
somebody was here with his girl.

"The living giggle in the dark all night,
And the dead are nothing."

I remember everything. On Easter
the women returned to Golgotha

to anoint him, but oh well
he was gone, left this Place

of Skull, reborn, looking
for his friends. Nobody believed

them, but everyone was paying
attention. And now it's another

sister. And so it tightens.
I swear I turned off the music

so I'd never miss a call.
I woke up at gate C21

Baltimore, C36 Denver—
I can do this daily, we'll

trade off, sleep with the phone,
change this job, find high-ceilinged

apartments. In April
I can fly anywhere. But really,

is it time yet? Let's look
at the moon that will keep us awake.

I'll ask my mother, Mary,
put in a word for us? Show

all your daughters what good
is it—who plants the sunflowers,

strolls summer evenings vibrant
with crickets; can you show us

if we'll ever make it home?
I don't get your togetherness.

If the bonds of dying fix
rigid before we're born

maybe you're praying for us—
now and at the hour of our deaths

"Teach us to care and not to care
Teach us to sit still,"

women running barefoot down
dusty roads, hardwood halls, all our potions

tossed, all our stupid notes.
At Newgrange they carved the rocks

infinity infinity. Who wins
the winter river ride?

I'm watching for a sign of rain.
I'm repeating this planting.

III

Summer

While it gets hazier and rainy as kingdoms, here I am
coolly hanging to see the truth of where it's taking me,
yanked into another muddy-sky midwestern
summer in paradise. I make no fine decisions 'til fall;
fine right now moans some near kind of dying
with you and with you and with you these midnights. I'm dreaming
all the time a story of a woman afraid her heart
does not happen, who will sing a Hail Mary
to put you to sleep. Don't need one; I'm not waking
from where I am with you here, it's this like kick drums,
I'm still laughing, she wants belief like eyes of a child
what fool what dignity, she believes it's coming back
with every lover she cuts off, each friend.
I got a, I got a fuchsia notion about sinks
and where you will be while I dream, so I'm dancing
in drizzle for more June, sleeping on the job for focus,
I do not want to know who someday
will write love songs, love songs. Fling me that t-shirt,
I might have to go find you in daylight, gone strange
and devastatingly emerald like peace.
I'll yowl to northern lights another day, I got
plans to get on highways and lawns, go tearing
through Target in hats with an angel called Rain
and I'm building a skyway out of my attic to clouds
for waiting like this, for patience,
defining such a thing as this, the heroics
before you wake.

No Deliberate Tributary

That is the thing about the river.
—Alan Dugan

To river; verb. Has something to do with
making people want you, making them
go away. Filtering out sticks, weeds,
canoes that got lost. Is a sloppy
action, can make you cold with collecting
like any breeze can raise your skin,
move out for heat. Rivering
has little to say about heat though, thinks
it's a person: A, B, and C wrapped up
and wrung out solid. A. Knows
more about others than about
self. B. Is always right
or can move further down
the current that is its definition.
Makes up definitions one day,
the next day, this is a new season.
Is not as smart as it thinks, acting toward
others, repeating old lives, old stories
about fishing trips, lily pads
with turtles on them, and many
kept, previously, supposedly, secrets until
only truth is left. C. Never wants to be alone
but *must* be. Be careful whom you river.
By the time it's finished you can't
get back to the beginning, can't
be certain what is the beginning, and whatever
branches off is always called
another name.

The Mirror to Deal With

The innocence of a child running inside
with a dandelion to his mother
makes me imagine someone telling him
You are the thing I can remember clearly
from the most hated part of my life.
What could this mean to a child? He
enters that door for me again and again
until all the dandelions are gone
and the house yellow,
aging paper.

Prove to me
like falling strips on the beautiful wall
what it means to record your life
in lipstick, Rosewood, on a mirror.
There is a signal everyone makes,
out of foil, tossed from a car window,
tossed without thought,
that no one ever notices. Prove
that you know what your signal means.
That you want to.

Pay attention to what has aged.
You can cover anything with flowers;
wilt, cascade, little ivories
of stupid luck. Try setting petals
on a mirror. Reconstruct them
with waxy diagrams, arrows and comments
to yourself like: sepal, first petals,
stamen inaccuracy here, a question mark,
begin again, begin everything again but
now, pay attention to what has aged.
Run with this somewhere,
without apology.

143 Smith Ave.

In the apartment downstairs at least three men live.
I'm thinking that they think I'm okay.
I feel them walk, they echo
my walking, maybe they listen
if I sing. We startle each other. Maybe

we see each other at the mailbox, maybe they
have a rhythm different from mine, mornings,
more mornings. They do. I think of them
as my men, one night I heard one's
girlfriend, my window was open above theirs

so I heard her like mercy.
I think I see people in time exposure;
the shutter closes, we are grown up. Oh.
My men climb their steps, outside my window
is a church, only feet from me, and nobody

goes there. Rather, two people do. Sunday mornings
one plays the upright piano, it echoes,
and somebody sings, sings to make up
for the echoes, and the Sundays clump
together, one, one after another.

Other Math

And she was the last light
from the marquee down the hill, the last
mud melting in front of the crack house or

the house of very short prayers.
In the morning, the snow memorizes.
The janitor is drunk

and singing the blues of his own morning
and all the nuns tuck themselves away, they use
the underground path to the cathedral where

a thought has texture, as if
you could hold it in your hand or take
it out of a pocket, collect it and re-

collect it, where you are never seen and where
the frost destroys the song of frost and passion,
the song of telling the truth,

the time it takes destroys
the time it takes,
the texture with gaps.

The nuns: The trees are dead now aren't
they? She was singing.
Delete. The gift to tell the truth and the way

the moon comes up over the city
the way the city comes. She is brilliant.
She is all you freeze over beginning

with *it feels like*—
You have selected, you
the cold sense it all makes

in the morning. It goes like:
She is her father
she is wherever it went.

Landlords, We Don't Just
Disappear into Those Homes

So you dream about this woman
every single night, well, morning,
to be precise—they're morning dreams.

The two of you stand in a huge field
with power lines and an empty road.
She tells you things:

All the husbands are away
in her town, the women hang
their laundry in backyards

and are finally beginning to plot.
The bachelors in town are curious,
but wary. She tells you

she was the best film-maker ever,
used another name, but gave it up.
Won't watch those films. Simply

the best. You want to ask about this
but she states it so simply
you believe her. In that yellow field

she's wiser than you. Some mornings
her hair is gray, the next she's in
a flowered dress, her hair blond,

she twirls in circles and her skirt
would make a cloudy parachute.
She laughs at your impeccable taste

for rain, you consider bringing her
things, some basil or four perfect
orange trees. You never bring

her anything; during the day
you never consider looking for her,
someone walking by, someone

you're falling in love with. You think
in the next dream you'll pin
her down, make her tell you

what she means; what did she mean
by saying the power lines carry
no message between any people?

Never ask. Never. She'll tell you
"I come to you so early in the morning
I never remember what I say."

She never remembers.
She never remembers.
She never remembers.

Rivera Live at Cyrano's

He had the piano. Night after night I'd
come and listen in that bar up the mountain, sit

with him who never saw me, as it turned
to snowing outside and his music told the story

of our lives together. A waiter and gin, the dry
light, not very much light, and the piano

telling me we would be unhappy, he
would demand more and more chords, a sadness

the best kind of sadness. I heard him. How
he could change, shifting to runs up and down

the roads that I drove to hear him, as if I
had him there. The perfect sadness that

he would leave me, leave me knowing he was
not free to go. That mountain was so odd.

At times it was all clear, the needles of trees
at the window pointed to snow and to

the next piece he'd play: Now we thank
ourselves, idiots, watch each other play

music that says it all comes out of that
music, are there lives behind those notes?

He never saw me, we never spoke and I thought
he was me. I could not say why he was not

frustrated, each night with all those questions:
You may never stop looking. How could

he play us as lovers? I am up and across roads
for him, I would give all my questions away

for one melody that never shifted, that never
held me so tightly I missed him over again.

Jeremy Rivera, give me all your talent, let me put
it away a while. I will give you sweaters, cold hands.

This Pulls on Choice

I could be wrong, but if I'm not
it's like this: With all the room
in this room I'm going to get a cold,
I've taken to looking at decorations,
a black jacket maybe, as significant,
and all the music I pick with nervousness
sounds the same, like rain might come. I seems
I want something, the floor seems like it,
it gets tiled or I paint it by accident,
and I'm trying, don't stop me, it might be

a warmer winter. If I wasn't wrong
it might be less pure gestures: No,
I will not harm anyone. You see, in fact,
I might. It isn't really warmer
on the floor, there isn't much rain left,
and I keep thinking I've got all
the time in the world for being wrong, do I
need to remember strong voices?

Once voice said Get out of my life, I hear
about deceit, about I am going
to want more, about *please*. There are
weird messages in new paint over blue,
one cup of cold coffee, one voice said
I will always love you. I'm going to get

—god, I'm going to get more tired? Quieter?
Whom do I keep safe when I say Yes,
now? It's not funny anymore when
I'm not really lonely; I only want
temporary choices. Whoever said we don't
have all the wrong timing we want?
We want better winters, we do not want a past,
my dangerous gesture is this:
It's not safe in this room.
Here.

It Never Comes Out of Nowhere

Here is how it was. We were just the two of us
there and into it and both, every now
and then, paused to listen. Don't you
think I didn't know it, think I didn't
stop too, when it was real hot on a couch
with the armrest bruising that bone back
of my neck where the head starts. I laughed
when I couldn't think where that bruise
came from next day, don't think I didn't know.

I will tell you what there is left
to say, I was listening then for fear,
like somebody in that room of you and me
was going to take it and I was afraid it would
be you. This is how it was. When a man's arm
jerks, he's asleep and you can do what you
want; don't think I never got any sleep,
that wasn't the only couch. I didn't. You

weren't listening anymore when that arm
would jerk and I got all the hearing. It said
No one remembers this. And I got it.
The one who sleeps will never be laughing
all that hard at me—what there is left to say
is what did you think you'd hear? This
is what you took: How can I think now
that I knew it was coming? I will take this
away from you, when you pause next, listen
like this: *You will not remember.*

Ruthless Use of Men
as Dictionaries

These men. What kind of idiot
do they think she is? The kind
who'd let her body dip
with them like she doesn't know what
it is to miss someone, or like
she'd be there tomorrow
waking up? Right there.
No. She misses, she loves,
but sometimes it's no big deal,
sometimes she just wants
to have her damned words defined.

Mary Magdalene Talks to Jesus on Holy Thursday

Well, what do you *think* I want?

I've got sand in my eyes, and look
at my feet, I been laying tar with them?
And it's not bad enough that I'm clueless
about what you're not even keeping quiet
about, but there are people taking a look
at me now. I hear it.
Mary Magdalene. Yeah, so?
So she got historical
'cause some guy she loved
got famous.

I'm not sure I've got it right anymore. I've got
your mother's broken heart, but she *likes* me,
she likes me a lot; I've got
pity from your nice friends,
I've got voices in my sleep saying
Oh Ms. Magdalene, why will you always make us say
Well, if you didn't know how to love him
you must've at least had a few good clues.

I've got no shoes.
I was always just sitting here can
I tell you this?
Your mother comes by,
she's so goddamned *sweet*,
to check if I'm okay, I mean
she feels sorry for me. If we
could all forget about history for once,
you know, she's a woman first.
She tells me how you talk about me.
She said you spoke of me before
all those seven demons, etc., you didn't say much,
just noticed me, like maybe you were glad
about those demons. In a way.
In another world.

I don't think it's as simple as this.
It doesn't come down to pity I don't want
and never needed—I was always just
here, can you tell them I never wanted
anything? No not you; you can't.
But I have, from time to time,
lived a life. I have gone hungry.
My hair is ratty like I got some crazy perm
at age 15 that won't go away, and I never
washed the feet of any man.
Not even you.

But it's not like that.
It's not a thing.
Maybe I wouldn't serve your old dinner tonight
not because I hate that but
because I don't know where the forks go,
because it has nothing to do with me
the way the horns blow at night
and call
to an earth.
I'm on the earth. My head
locks to it every night.
But all I can get, sweating there, insomniac,
is that you're *wrong*.

How's it going to be that good?
I figured years ago
if someone wants to try to save the world
you have to let him.
But sometimes it's
a real world.
Sometimes it gets cool at night
and you're laughing your head off
and your chin needs touching
or kids are telling you about
the dream they have of the dog they have

that lives forever in the dream
and they wake up and still have
that dog,
or your mother tells you
to stop working so hard,
not out of her niceness
but because you're driving her nuts
tromping into town at midnight,
never saying good-bye when you leave.
Because you smile at her then.

What will I do
with your mother?
You forget all that; you forget how much
what you're really doing is
leaving us behind.
Watering the plants.
Disciplining the cats; you can't, even you
can't make it stop.
And I don't get it anymore.
'Cause we all know what's coming
and the sun blazes, the moon burns
there is wheat and skin
and more and more wine—
it's big.
It's real big.
So all I can see is your glass of water,
my cigarettes, the way night falls
and filters lights all over the place.
The tops of houses are warm.
My mouth is dusty.
I think you're insane I just
don't see it that large and
not strange, not slaughtered
and gone, simply,
the gut of my stomach
begs only.

And so I listen for a while, crickets,
the ticking of your thinking, sad, about this night,
it all; there's a scenario I play:
The 10-year-old girls sing
the movie song
to some kid with big eyes
and I come and say it all—
I say *It Does Matter.*
It's worth history and pity
and the way mothers say
When a woman screams she is a child,
when a man cries he is your son.
The way they are somebody's mother.
I come to the 10-year-old girls
and say that I did too
know how to love him—
if someone, anyone, would've stopped feeling bad
for the pure unrequitedness of that love
they would've seen it was perfect.
How I never had to make a choice.
How I never even got to be bad.
How one night you sat there and told me a story
that had *no meaning,*
how you just *liked* that story.
What you look like coming into town
when it's first getting dark and I've been here
for so long with nobody to beat me at trivia games
and you're looking so tired
'cause you *walked* here, for god's sake,
and I think to myself this time,
this time I will run down the street
over the glass and the oil and the dogs right
through them all and wham you in a hug
in front of everyone, and it's going to mean

please.
You lunatic wanderer.
It gets so good down here.

But the little girls are melancholy.
They start singing again, knowingly, and pat my hand.
They ask about your mother 'cause she
was really a hero, or she was
a something. They bring her lilacs.
I don't think I would've had
daughters like these.

I don't think sadness
matters that much.
What'll always break my heart is hope—
the way a kid smiles at a girl
in white with flowers at his mother's funeral,
the way men leave the lights on at night,
the fact that stories get told, and how
you did what you did 'cause you *wept*, once,
and yes, I don't think you're really all that tough.
Maybe you can't make guys who love you
betray you.
Maybe you're going to scream out tomorrow
and I won't come.
Maybe you're just trying not to ever
see anybody die, or really
you refuse to ever watch anyone survive.

Sometimes this world doesn't need saving.
The clouds passing over the moon look exactly
like the ocean at night, couples talk about
the funny thing they said yesterday for days.
My clothes are destroyed

and smell like salt.
I've got a runny nose from never sleeping
and I will drink more wine than ever
and if you really pull this thing off
you come to *me*.
I'm not your mother.

And if I love you, you crazy, wrecked bastard,
then there's more pity than what
would ever just
pity us.

IV

Backyards in
Sligo Town

The coiled cats stare
at each other from wall
to wall, the rain

slunk now south
to Lough Gill, the mist
sits like shed fur snagged
on these startling trees.

Only April, but you
can barely see
the blasted ancient
walls, round shouldered,

the alleys wooded over
like some sylvan comic
between the yards, tight

for clotheslines, coconut-
scented bushes, leaves
and antique raised doorways—

the same passages
you knew then. On Upper
Johns Street the kids
who danced and curled

at the cathedral's Annual
Teen Night are now
in love, these kisses against
the whitewash all pelvis

are not the first. We look
away, my sisters and I.
We shut the windows to sleep.

Margaret McCormick,
we're never going to find you
in Sligo. You left
too young and alone

in the 1880s.
We're careful clambering
through this greenery

and watch for your pence
tossed into the Garavogue
off looped Hyde Bridge,

your wishes spanning oceans
still coming true for you—
we know better than
to ever forget our dead:

stumbling, damaged. We try
to be great-granddaughters.
We know where everyone

is buried. Under Ben Bulben
we see the fields, stone walls,
the plot for each farmhouse,

the row houses in town and
two-story shops on O'Connell.
We almost catch you

at ruined Sligo Abbey,
the crumbly 13th century
palace misty-romantic then
to the 16-year-old Margaret

who got on the boat
with Sligo girls quick, smart
and permanent.

The trees and bushes overtake
the lanes. The cars park
where they can.

We're going back to Sligo.
Nothing has changed
since you fled.

Rural Conductors

1
My father was an engineer.
He jogged long distance.
He kept journals,
recording the date and mileage
of 20 years of running
in lined stenographer notebooks.
He tracked weekly averages,
the total miles reached in each
type of running shoe, things like
temperature, time of day, altitude's
affect on distance.

2
Along rural Wisconsin roads
clover fills ditches sweet pink
in the spring, and the black tar
spits pebbles down the long grass.
The earth is spongy under the road.
Frogs sing in the cattails
where redwing blackbirds
occasionally sway.

3
I never read the journals.
My father's bride
would not lend them to me
when he died of cancer.
Instead I read a novel
as I sat in vigil
his last week that April
in Fresno, California.
The hero in my book
lay in a hospital bed
hallucinating away the pain
from a gunshot wound, surrounded

by narratively tight ghosts,
strong lyrical prose and the pure
love of smitten readers.

My father dreamt and woke,
told me the colors of his pain-killers,
the in-and-out narcotic conversations
of the doomed. We smiled.
I got him more ice chips.

4
The back roads twisting
near Yosemite, California,
wind and slither through razor-
sharp grass past plots of hard-edged
crops: olives, pistachios, rosemary,
the colors of adulthood.
The dust rises from gravel
and coats shoes red.

5
I've had other Aprils.
A boy once loved me
some other springtime.
Everybody knows I
keep my letters.
Along the bike paths
and parkways of Minneapolis
violets struggle from underneath bushes,
squirrels flash out of the brush
right into your ankles;
Canadian geese rise and squawk
to move you along.
I plant pansies in window boxes
for luck.

6

In the Midwest in winter
the high-voltage electric
transmission lines that cross
these flat white fields
during ice storms sometimes
get coated solid with ice,
the wind whips them
and jangles them until
they beat over and over
a staggered harsh pattern
hard, from pole to pole.
The engineers call this
galloping conductors.
Outages are widespread.

The Prairie

Jan takes me driving out
to Sullivan's Wood nature
sanctuary and prairie
restoration west straight

away from Lake Winnebago—
corn land, dirt farms and hickory;
she takes Milwaukee
city kids here for tours,

they plant little bluestem,
hang wood-carved signs with all
the plant names, and yearly she
counts the sandhill cranes.

She's with the Audubon
and the Sierra and with all
those who know and know. Jan
was my mother's tennis

partner; they aced the city
courts in the '70s, Jan
had down the intimidation
psych-outs; my mother

a wicked serve, and for me,
neither any on-court mercy.
The annual crane count
is at 4:30 a.m.

Jan has to be there.
Each counter is assigned clear
area to cover, and if any
sandhill cranes fly there

you count them as yours.
The rookery lurks
alongside the cornfield—
giant black shreddy

nests perch way above
reason. It's not leafy yet
in June. Sandhill cranes
stand over five feet tall,

wingspan over six. How
they roost on slim branches
with mates and young and all
I don't know. They like

to eat the corn. In Sullivan's Wood
we see wild iris, prairie dock and compass;
Jan teaches me the warble
the mated crane makes, she shows

me mayapple and New England aster
gone rare long ago.
There are folks who know how
to bring everything back.

And suddenly, we hear it:
the loopy candy flutter
of the crane and there!
One by one, long-neck dinosaur

heads pop above the corn
and heavily, staggered, they finally fly,
brown swollen globes on necks.
I count 12.

Monona Terrace

*Architecture might extend the bounds
of human individuality indefinitely
by way of safe interior discipline.*
    —Frank Lloyd Wright

I was a teenager in Madison.
It was summer—
cigarettes on docks
over Mendota, painters' easels,
sailboats' slow crawl,

Frank Lloyd Wright homes
strange and mad
straight out of the soil,
snuggled to high-atticked
neighbors, vain bay windows.

There was a boy, music,
pages of scores he scribbled
like timed math tests,
plastic chairs right-hand

surface, smooth blank
symphony sheets,
he filled in line after line
like transcription—
any key, any instrument.

I watched through
the gauze of being 16,
the mist of my half-ounce,
the weight of this

my mother's hometown,
my mother was dying,
her past becoming
my history, his future
becoming curious

half note by half note,
adagio, andante, allegro,
I could not read even
at the rate he wrote,

to him simple numbers,
blankness of pages—
the world right there
in octaves, all souls eight notes,

the passing of a day,
time kept from the toe back
to the heel of your foot,
quick motions like splinters,
arcs of beveled glass,

the complex and concentrated,
the raised eyebrow,
the places you watch a mind go
away beyond wanting to.

Hot tiled corridors,
sweaty auditions,
waiting sitting on the floor,
results and rehearsals,

vending machine hum,
damp slog through woods,
plank docks and moon and this
his balance, cut time,

straight out of the soil,
buried clean.
Bikes and textbooks,
sandwiches, the muddle

then of adulthood
unpredictable in poverty
planed away strange,
surfacey, barlit and sad.
I was finding the drinkers.

If I am ever 16 again
I will take him with me
into that dread silent
house of loss. When you're

a child you must find
the otherworldly.
It will never come back.
But it was nothing. It was children.

One time at Maricopa dorm,
I kissed him.
I remember I was drunk
but I meant it.

I end up in Madison now.
I spend this strange time here
with the dead. I get lost,
drive for hours, spot art,
old homes, bay windows.

In 1938 Frank Lloyd Wright
designed a convention center
for Lake Monona.
It opened in 1997.

I never stop thinking of you,
you know. It's here—

a wish that you are well,
that you made good
on that promise,

dose of some grace,
that you had the angel
we hope touches someone.
Midwestern frozen earth,
stumbling shocks stun

us oblivious again.
Someone is composing
these personal soundtracks.
I look for you. It's watery.

It Might Be Deep Blue

I was 16, my mother cooked noodles, I
was waiting, watching her stir, shut drawers, hold
up a small strainer. Which I've inherited
from my son, she says, dumps steam and soupy
strands into it. My brother's marijuana strainer,
I see, idly wonder where all the fragments
of his deep blue bong have gone. So blue
it had been a sin sitting on the kitchen table
five days ago, after school. She thought it was
a vase for flowers at first it was so blue, and she
so odd about us. My brother gone, only I knew
where he lived and I wasn't telling, it broke
her heart, I think. Maybe she'd read
about drug abuse, maybe she believed
everything. Snowy nights under quilts with the windows
wide open, mornings watching me play the piano,
my brother on the couch mildly curious
about creating; I told her once then that each
person had to create himself—my father
in his rancher hat and boots, her always wanting
to create, yet thinking my father odd. She never,
I think, stopped thinking of her children as *her*,
could not survive our errors. Nobody
was wrong, nobody. Those blue chips
held up to a light, Mother, might show you
anything, might mean passage, might mean a new
kind of greatness. I was 16, that night she gripped
my hand on my bed, wept I miss him can
he come back yet?
I said no.

Maggy, 1984

From the room next door comes the sound, softly
pinning my arms to my sides and eyelids open,
of a girl crying into Kleenex. She is my sister
and it's dark and the damp moonlight shows me swirls
in the plaster on our wall; the edges of the circles
make the sound of sniffing and catch their breath.
I'm guilty of being happy in the same place,
the same life, that she hates like the heat in the air
hates the moisture that traps it to the bodies of people who
can only lie and wait for the sweat to dry.

I want to tell her things will be fine soon
but a part of me has melted onto the bed, into
a way of thinking that she doesn't know, and one that
isn't sure anymore what things are fine for her.
Her hair is short now; it has nothing to do with me
in the same way that the breeze which finally
eases in my window also touches her and leaves.

In Memoriam

As we were all leaving you spoke no more,
I cannot see with my left eye.
For a long time. I waited
I wait
I have been waiting
but not like the way you sang once
in a garden, smelling rhubarb leaves, and we,
the goddamned in lettuce, singing Here
I am. With my head tilted to the side
I may see the half of the sun
that is out, the sides of buildings
you said it would be okay as if
in the beginning, is now, and
my only eye aches,
the wind
isn't a real world, isn't any
old world, rain comes right in the window,
touches some face, the wrong side
of that face, which,
it would let you slap it.
Halfway to you
before children run
screaming at each other in a field
because it needs to,
because they can feel it,
you start in one hand, that elbow,
that shoulder; you offer
have been
she offers me
used to, now,
and at the hour
in that hour: What ages
are your children now?

Stopping at Riverside

First they stab your hip—
the harvest, they call it;

they trundle off your marrow
to the deep freeze for chemo

and then they dose you
so hard it dissolves every

mucous membrane in you.
You're in the ward five weeks.

Every day one door shuts
and we see that family in the hall,

crying. We give them our extra
paper flowers. We wash hands.

I come to Riverside Cemetery
to see my family. Do you know

what happened the day I left
your ward? I never believed

it wasn't being done to me.
So I lost my immunity

and it never comes back.
We have three new markers

at Riverside. Two of you
in cenotaph. The Fox River trips

past, the seagulls pause on the docks.
We love the secrets of ashes,

the clean wash of lake water
like all the nights we sat

with the little waves lapping.
We filled your hospital room

floor to ceiling with color, hand crafts,
posters and lights. Hello; come in.

I know where you landed.
I can't bear to be out here alone.

Sometimes I think that I've caught it.
Remember: I can't do it like you did,

so catch me when I slink into the Fox
off the Oshkosh Avenue bridge.

I will bring you a family portrait—
this is what we look like now.

Dignity in the Home

All the chairs and the long brown couch just lay
down on the floor in a line and the thin
curtains joined them, sort of on the side
or fluttering down onto them and I watched
thinking this is the kind of loneliness I
should've known about and this is nonsense: I object.
But the furniture line was so heavy
it went right out the door and some of my
neighbors' lamps joined in, the tails
of extension cords and paths of towels and bedding
went straight down the lawn to the lake where
even my toothbrush and coffee mug with the cats
on it had slunk, so dejected it didn't
even matter they were in the water with some
cold rocks and a clam. All were loaded down
with the despair so poignant in furnishings, each
I tried to coax back into the house, gathering
the alarm clock and frying pan from the lake,
but, almost politely, they moved from
my hands back down to that cold home
with the fierce clam, who guarded them
from my confusion. They were so quiet
about it, I loved them. My pajamas floated
with such purpose, reached for the laces of one of my
old tennis shoes out nearly to the reef,
reached without expectation.

Music

A man played two chords on
an old grand piano
in his living room, played them
over and over, F major,
D minor.
You could ask him why, but you could see
he was trying to figure it out.
This took a kind of energy.
This took the kind you would direct
to a place you called home—
maybe wherever you were born,
maybe the kind you keep in reserve
while you understand the pure things:
an avocado
—all, I think, in the list.
The man, it's clear, hopes to add
his chords to the list.

Do you really want to ask about music?
Melodies fall, leaves fall, you
will receive letters from old friends and think,
How could it have been two years?

The avocado, when presented as a gift,
means love.

Notes

"Rage": The italicized section in the ninth stanza is from *Histoire et mémoires de la Société Royale de Médecine,* v.6 (1783), second observation by M. Minot (1781, p. 50), translated from the French by Maggy Brown.

"Necedah, Wisconsin—12/24/96" : This poem is for Mark Miller (1962–1996).

"Easter" : The quotation at the end of section 1 is a misquote of the last two lines of "Listening to the Mourners" by James Wright. The first set of quotations in Section 5 is from "At the Grave" by James Wright. The second set of quotations in Section 5 is from "Ash Wednesday" by T. S. Eliot.

"Stopping at Riverside" : This poem is modeled on "To the Muse" by James Wright.

"Allusive, edgy, smart, and utterly relentless, the poems of *Year of Morphines* move gracefully in the zone between our necessary morphine spells of forgetting and life's implausible reclamations: ' . . . all these stories ending with life.'"

    —GEORGE GARRETT, FROM HIS JUDGE'S CITATION

Betsy Brown is no stranger to loss. Breast cancer runs rampant in her family; both her mother and her thirty-two-year-old sister died of the disease, and another sister has been diagnosed with its late stages. Her father also fell victim to cancer, this time pancreatic. The poems in Brown's stunning first book pivot around the mechanisms we use in facing loss and fear—whether those confrontations are as wrenching as a bone marrow transplant or as confused as a brief love. An unusually intimate collection, *Year of Morphines* is both a heartbreaking portrait of the process of death and encouraging evidence of life's perseverance.

"A moving, merciless, and incomparably lovely collection."
    —DAVID FOSTER WALLACE

"In *Year of Morphines,* Betsy Brown, faced with immense grief, creates brilliant, original poems, evoking her midwestern youth and the eventual shattering of her family. But it is her powerful images and insights that make these poems sing and stay with you. There are poems here, such as 'Dignity in the Home,' that I will never forget."
    —JAMES TATE

A native of Oshkosh, Wisconsin, BETSY BROWN works in corporate communications in Minneapolis.

Cover illustration: *Portal,* by Georgia Mason

LOUISIANA STATE UNIVERSITY PRESS
Baton Rouge 70803

ISBN 0-8071-2783-3

9 780807 127834

90000>

Printed in U.S.A.

$16.95

THE
ALL-PURPOSE
MAGICAL
TENT

LYTTON
SMITH